Corona Kindness

Alice King

Produced by Softwood Books
Office 2, Wharfisde House, Prentice Road, Suffolk, IP14 1RD

First Edition

Paperback ISBN: 978-1-0687063-0-1

www.softwoodbooks.com

Mums and dads

children Postal Delivery Services

Doctors + Nurses

family and friends

families

Newly-weds

our pets

Everyone

hairdressers

Scientists

THANK

Teachers

YOU!

Sir Tom

FOOD BANKS

CHARITIES

Local businesses   parents

Joe   W'icks

brides and grooms

all the Staff

babies

Thank You!

This book is dedicated to the real heroes of the Coronavirus Pandemic. A 'Thank You' doesn't quite seem enough for what you did, but I hope this book in some way thanks you for your amazing, inspiring, and truly irreplaceable acts of kindness.

There is an endless list of people we need to thank: doctors, nurses, delivery drivers, parents, children, grandparents, families, friends, charity workers, shop keepers, scientists, Joe Wicks, Sir Tom..... along with countless others I could not squeeze into this book.

I felt I had to write this book to celebrate the kindness of people and to remind us that there will always be light and kindness even in the darkest parts of our lives. The illustrations in this story are based on real experiences and events.

*

Thank you to my Mum, Dad, Sister, Grandparents (age 80+), friends: Megan, Grecia, Faith, Lois, Elise, Erin, Jared, Holly, Saskia, Xander (ages 21 26), Eddie (age 8), Sarah, Elise (age 6), Harry, Robert, Paul, Rob and Wilfred (8months).

Thank you for inspiring and handwriting these pages and thank you for being a part of this book!

Thank You x

To all the brides and grooms who had to alter, or put their weddings on hold.

To all the Newly-weds who had to postpone their dream honeymoons and settle for something more normal.

To all the parents who taught their children how to social distance.

Thank you!

To Sir Tom,
    Thank you for inspiring us all. Your brave steps helped us realise we should never give up.

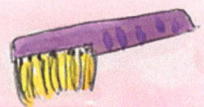

To the hairdressers,
Thankyou for welcoming us back
with open arms, despite our
'interesting' new lockdown locks!

To our pets who suddenly endured an unusual amount of love and attention. Thank you for putting up with us!

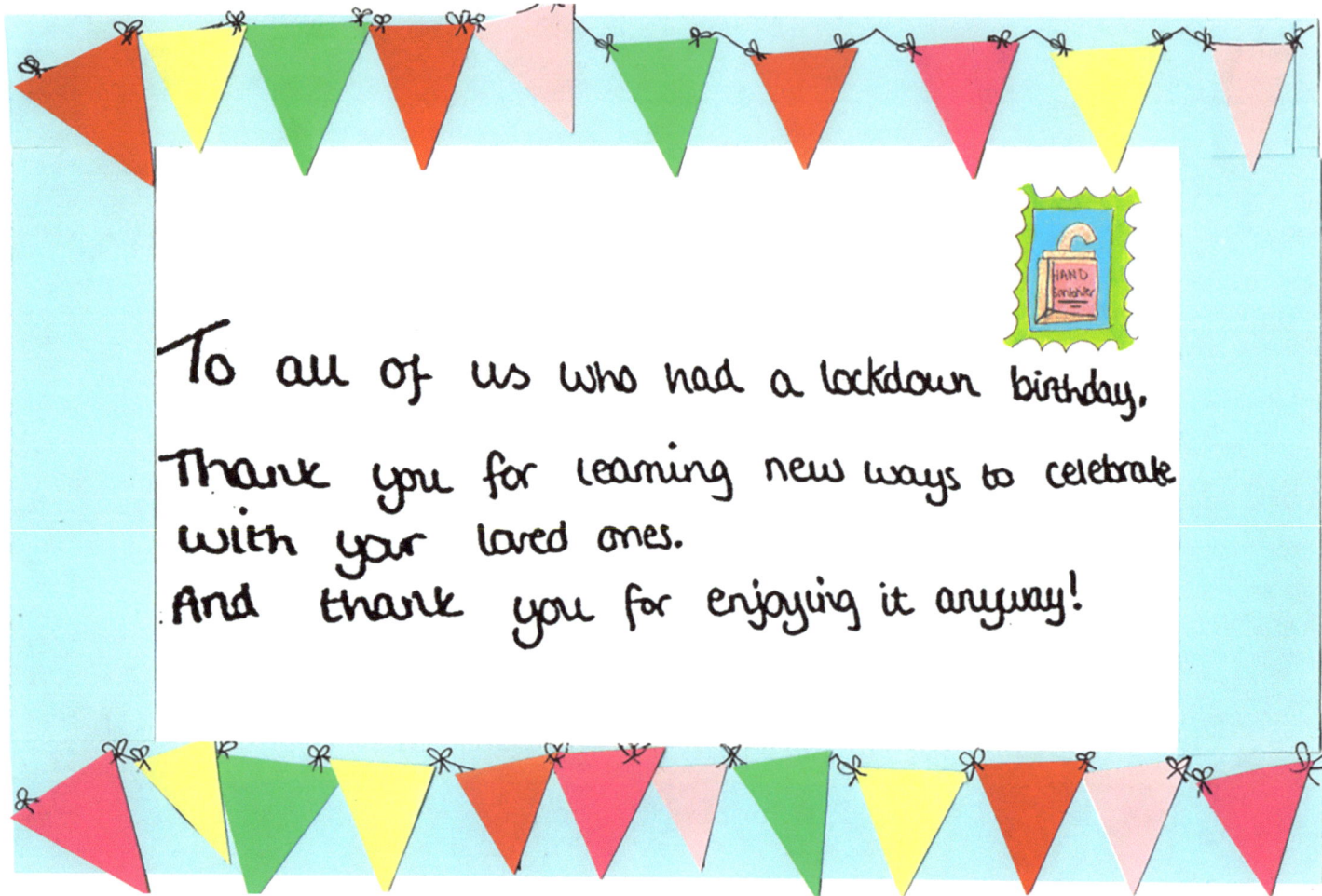

To all of us who had a lockdown birthday,

Thank you for learning new ways to celebrate with your loved ones.
And thank you for enjoying it anyway!

TO ALL THE
Doctors + Nurses
~thank you~

FOR WORKING ENDLESS HOURS,
PUTTING YOURSELF AT RISK +
CONTINUING TO LOOK AFTER US.

P.S.
thank you for making
your masks and PPE less
scary for kids, by adding
photos and funny characters.

thank you!

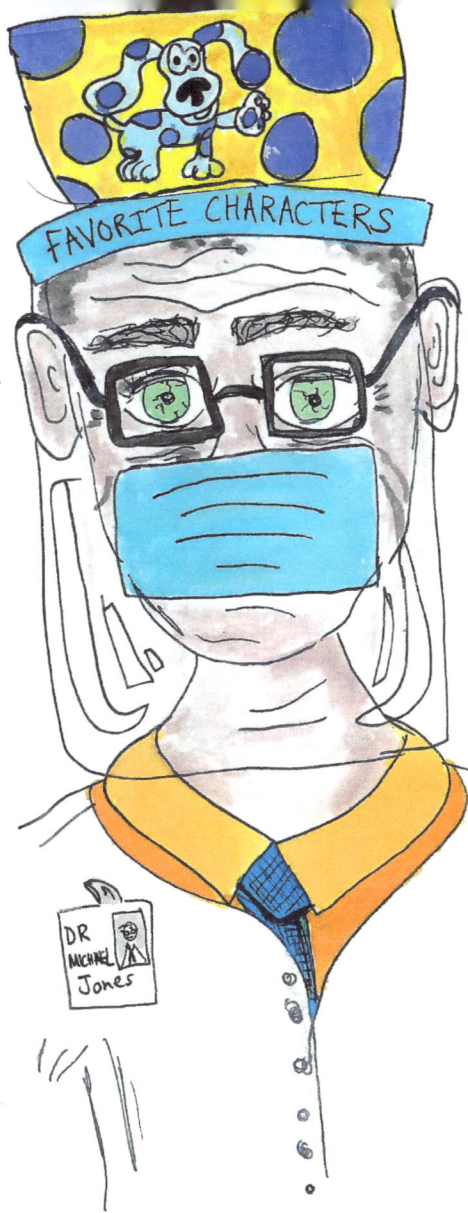

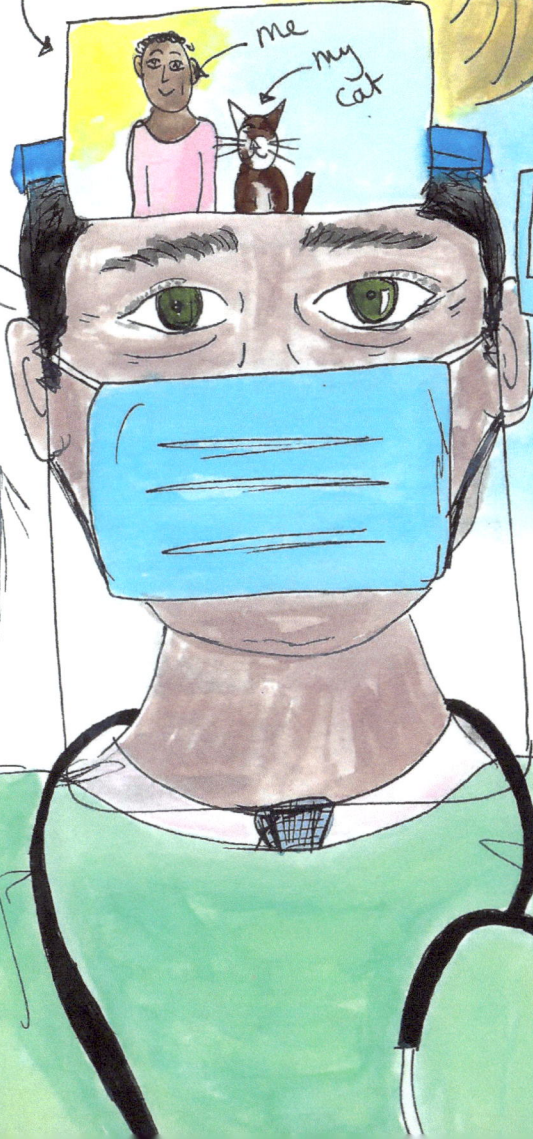

To Everyone who Kept
Themselves Busy during
Lockdown. Well done for
distracting yourselves

Putting on Shows

OUR SHOW

AMAZING
That was the best show yet!
What a show!

Playing Games

Learning New Skills

ITALIAN
Hello - buongiorno

TV

N

POP CORN

Gardening

IMPROVEMENTS

PAINT

To all the scientists who worked endlessly to find a cure.

To all the new Mums and dads who had to learn to be parents without the help and guidance from their families and friends.

... and to all the babies who were born during the Coronavirus pandemic who had only be held in their parents' arms.

To the people who isolated from their own families so that they could put themselves at risk to help others.

To the local businesses who had to close, but decided to use their leftovers for good. They put their profits to one side and just helped.

To our family and friends.
Thank you for being there for
us when we suffered from
the lockdown lows.
Thank you for lifting us back
up and for bringing the light
back into our lives.

To all the staff who worked in the shops,
Thank you for keeping the shelves stocked. :)

To our families who Face Timed us and allowed us to watch our grandchildren, nieces and nephews grow from behind a screen. Thank you for making us feel a little less apart.

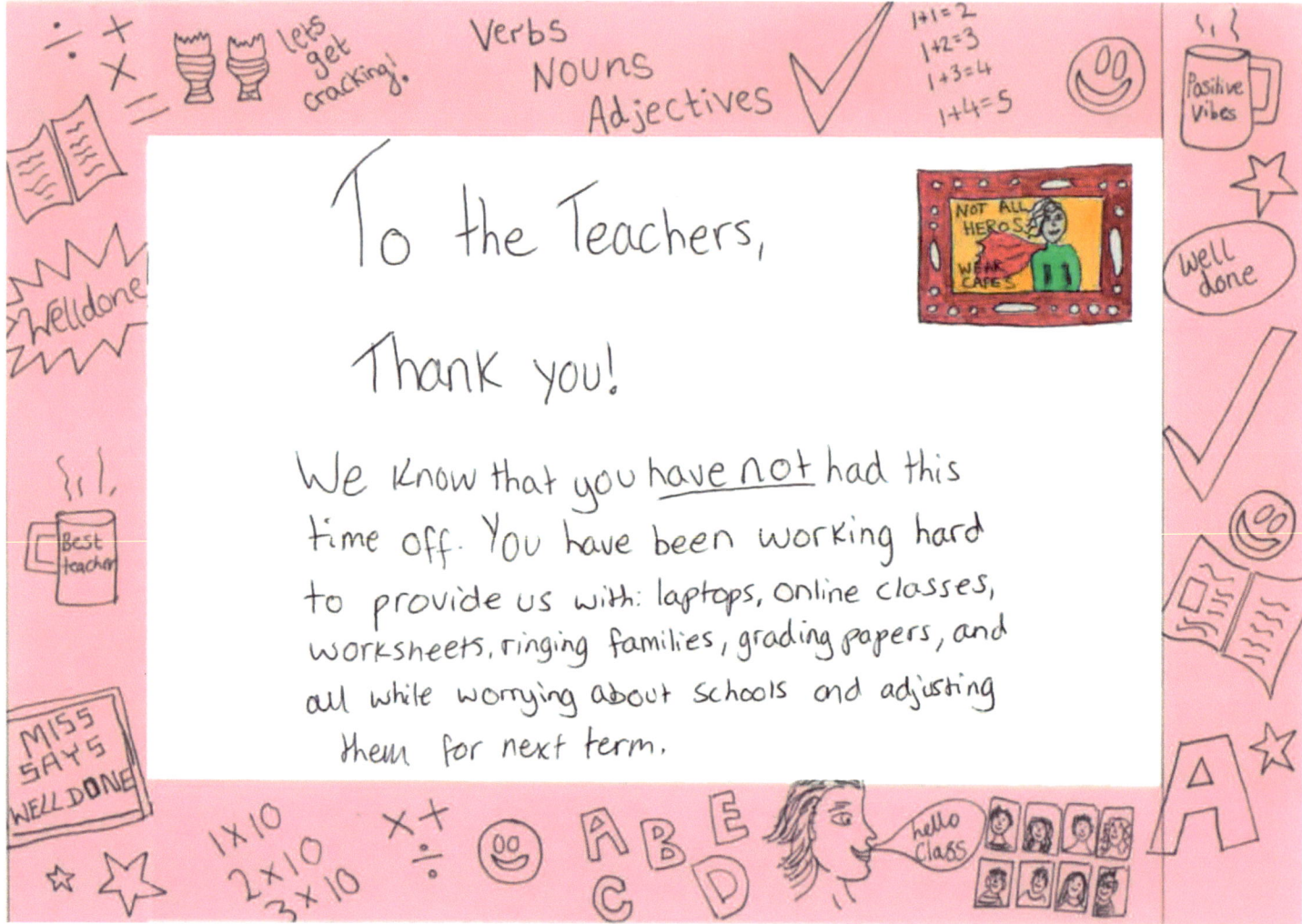

To the Teachers,

Thank you!

We know that you have not had this time off. You have been working hard to provide us with: laptops, online classes, worksheets, ringing families, grading papers, and all while worrying about schools and adjusting them for next term.

EXPECTATION   Reality

To Everyone,

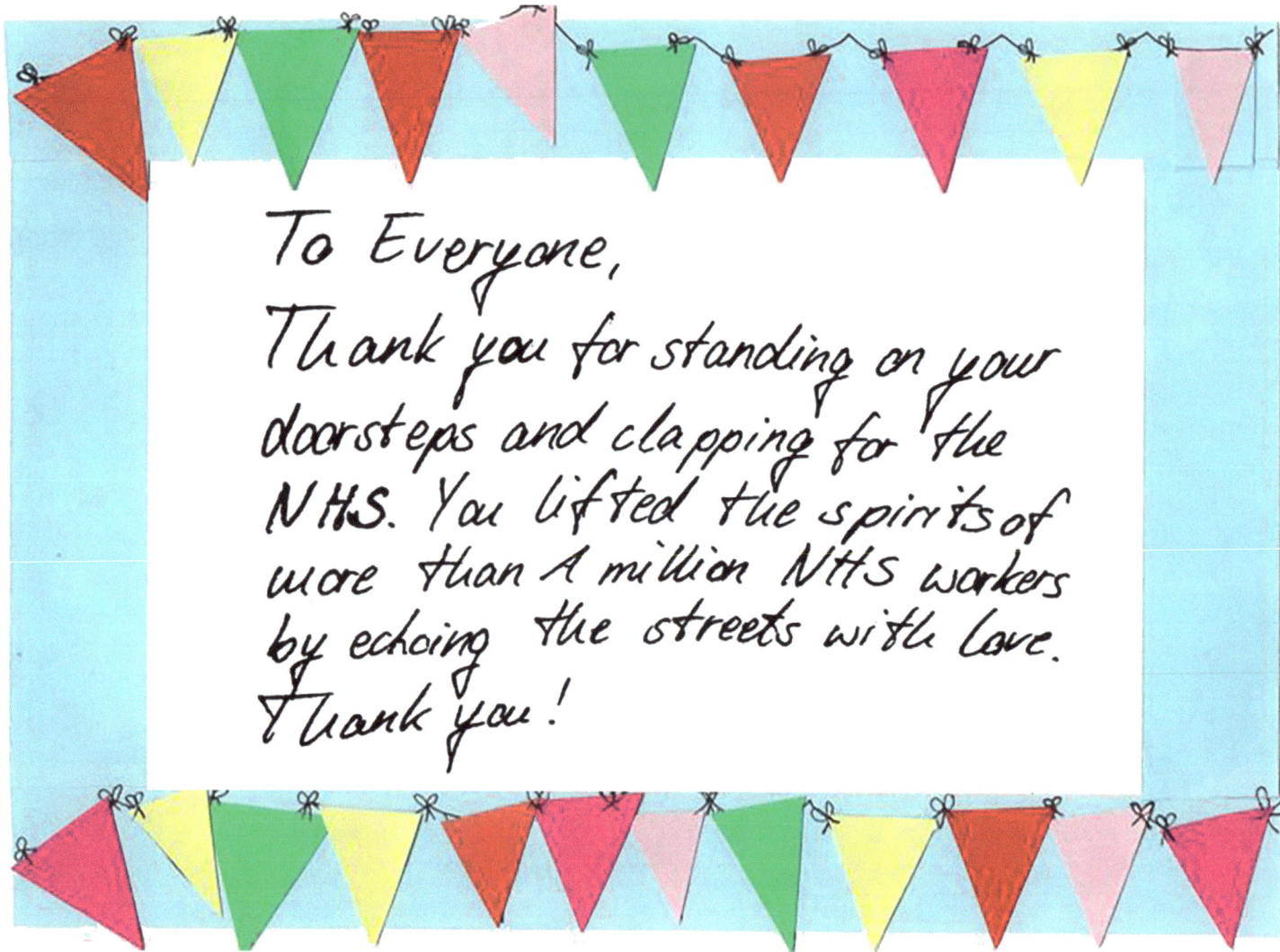

Thank you for standing on your doorsteps and clapping for the NHS. You lifted the spirits of more than a million NHS workers by echoing the streets with love.

Thank you!

And THANK YOU!

www.ingramcontent.com/pod-product-compliance
Lightning Source LLC
Chambersburg PA
CBHW041949080426

42735CB00004B/143